Education by Windows

ALSO FROM POETS & TRAITORS PRESS

Advances in Embroidery by Ahmad Al-Ashqar
Relative Genitive by Val Vinokur

Education by Windows

JOHNNY LORENZ

poems with translations from Mario Quintana

Copyright © 2018 by Johnny Lorenz and Poets & Traitors Inc.
All rights reserved.

Prior publication acknowledgements appear at the beginning of this text.
Cover image and design: Bernie DeChant

Published 2018 in New York by Poets & Traitors Press
www.poets-traitors.com
poetstraitors@gmail.com

Editors: Val Vinokur, Gili Ostfield
Editorial Advisors: Stephanie Leone, Rebekah Smith, Raúl Rubio

Published in the United States of America

Poets & Traitors Press is an independent publisher of books of poetry and translations by a single author/translator. The press emerged from the Poet/Translator Reading Series and from the New School's Literary Translation Workshop to showcase authors who travel between writing and translation, artists for whom *Language* is made manifest through *languages* and whose own word carries, shapes, and is shaped by that of another.

Poets & Traitors Press acknowledges support from Melissa Friedling, Stephanie Browner, Raúl Rubio, Alex Draifinger, Jane McNamara, Eugene Lang College, the New School Bachelor's Program for Adults and Transfer Students, and the New School Foreign Languages Department.

ISBN: 978-0-9990737-2-8

for Meaghan and Caetano and Fiamma

ACKNOWLEDGMENTS

Versions of the following poems have been published previously: "Brown Paper Bag," *Quiddity*, Volume 5.1, Spring/Summer 2012; "The Rubber-Tapper's Wife" and "Blackout in Sapucaia do Sul," *Luso-American Literature*, Rutgers University Press, 2011; "Love Letter to the IMF" and "Rain Diary," *Rattapallax* 13, 2006; "Education by Windows," *The Massachusetts Review*, Volume 46.3, Fall 2005; "Hortênsias," *maquina do mundo: revista de poesia*, 2005; "São Leopoldo," *Filling Station*, Issue 24, April 2002.

The translation of Mario Quintana's "The Map" ("O Mapa") originally appeared in *Metamorphoses*, Volume 16.2, Fall 2008, and the translations of "Parable?" ("Parábola?") and "Sadness of Writing" ("Tristeza de Escrever") appeared in *Bitter Oleander*, Volume 14.2, Autumn 2008. The translation of "Little Protest Poem" ("Poeminho do Contra") appears in my essay "Traduzindo pássaros: Os epigramas de Mario Quintana," forthcoming in *História Geral do Rio Grande do Sul: A Literatura*, Editora Méritos.

I am extremely grateful to the Fulbright Scholar Program for supporting my translations of Quintana's poetry. I am grateful, too, to UNISINOS (São Leopoldo, RS, Brazil) and especially Profa. Adila Beatriz Naud de Moura for hosting me during my Fulbright and to the Archive of Mario Quintana, which, at the time, was directed by Profa. Maria da Glória Bordini at PUC-RS. Permission to publish translations of Quintana's poetry was made possible through the generosity of Agência Riff and Elena Quintana Oliveira. I would also like to thank my home institution, Montclair State University, for its support, and my students for their inspiration.

Finally: thank you, thank you, dear friends.
Agradeço a minha família, que é a minha força.

CONTENTS

Preface

i. *there are so many consolations*

5   Love Letter to the IMF
6   Enter the Dragon
7   Machine
8   Saffron
10   479
11   The Borrowed Chapel
12   Brown Paper Bag
14   The Night I Turned to Water
16   Mourning Dove's Meter
18   Child
19   Poem for Michael K.
20   I Turned my Back on Words
21   Prayer to San Lazaro de Monsanto
22   Dreaming in Portuguese
23   Blade

ii. Poems by Mario Quintana (translated by J. Lorenz)

26   *Parábola?* / Parable?
26   *Texto & Pretexto* / Text & Pretext
26   *Do Sonho* / Of Dreams
26   *Evolução* / Evolution
28   *Tristeza de Escrever* / Sadness of Writing
28   *Os Intermediários* / The Intermediaries
28   *Da Saudade* / Of Longing
28   *Circo* / Circus
30   *Tempo* / Time
30   *Um Pouco de Geometria* / A Little Geometry
30   *Fé* / Faith
30   *Da Infinita Solidão* / Of Infinite Solitude
32   *Ars Longa* / Ars Longa

32 *Prosódia* / Prosody
32 *O Tempo* / Time
32 *Urbanística* / Urbanistic
34 *O Poema* / The Poem
34 *Exame de Inconsciência* / Self-examination
34 *E Daí?* / So?
34 *O Humilde Tesouro* / Humble Treasure
36 *Sonho de Uma Noite de Verão* / A Midsummer Night's Dream
36 *O Supremo Castigo* / Supreme Punishment
38 *Se o Poeta Falar num Gato* / If the Poet Were to Speak of a Cat
38 *A Lua de Babilônia* / The Moon of Babylon
38 *O Espectador* / The Spectator
40 *O Umbigo* / Belly Button
40 *Poeminho do Contra* / Little Protest Poem
40 *Da Realidade* / Of Reality
42 *Do Espetáculo desta Vida* / Of the Spectacle that is Life
42 *Da Discrição* / Of Discretion
42 *Das Utopias* / Of Utopias
42 *Da Paz Interior* / Of Inner Peace
44 *Da Vergonha* / Of Shame
44 *Da Inquieta Esperança* / Of Restless Hope
44 IV "*Minha rua está cheia de pregões*" / "I hear the delights the vendors are selling"
46 V "*Eu nada entendo da questão social*" / "What does the 'social question' mean?"
46 VI "*Na minha rua há um menininho doente*" / "The boy who lives nearby is ill"
48 XVII "*Da vez primeira em que me assassinaram*" / "The first time that they murdered me"
48 XXIII "*Cidadezinha cheia de graça*" / "I even pity this little town"
50 *O Mapa* / The Map
52 *Carta* / Letter

iii. *they gave me wine*

61 Postcards from the Labyrinth
63 The Rubber-Tapper's Wife
64 Rain Diary
66 Hortênsias / Hydrangeas
68 The Vase in the Maple
69 The Word "Quintessential"
70 São Leopoldo
71 Landscapes Without Poetry
72 Precision
73 Your House Without You
74 The Bath
76 Blackout in Sapucaia do Sul
77 The V
78 Baby Rat
79 Education by Windows
80 Sebastian
81 Writing
84 Carnaval

Education by Windows

PREFACE

I was born and raised in the United States.
My parents hail from Brazil.

But these countries are ideas; they are not places.
Cities, perhaps, are places.

I grew up in Miami Beach, a ribbon of condos on the edge of a continent. A city where English is not sufficient.

I lived, for a little while, in the south of Brazil, in a city called Porto Alegre—the adopted city of the poet Mario Quintana.

Dear reader, imagine asking random pedestrians: *Who is the poet of your city?*

Could they answer you? In Porto Alegre, everyone knows who Mario Quintana is. While I was living there as a Fulbright scholar, a waiter noticed one of Quintana's books on my table; he proceeded to recite Quintana's poetry to me. On another occasion, a late-night taxi driver kept chatting with me about Quintana long after I had paid the fare. When an airport luggage handler learned I was in Brazil to translate Quintana, he bought me a cup of coffee.

I was a professor returning to the land of his family; the good son who came home, even if it wasn't home; the translator who would bring Quintana's work from Brazilian Portuguese into American English. I offer it here, in this book, nestled between two sections of my own poetry.

At a time when the American education system continues to downplay or aggressively dismantle secondary language education, when immigrants are constantly framed as economic and cultural problems or even criminalized, those of us who speak more than one language understand that it is a gift to move between systems. And to be keenly aware of the limits of any of these systems.

This is the shared work of poets and translators: to meditate on the silence just beyond what can be said.

—Johnny Lorenz

i.

The boy looked up at the night sky
and said to his father:
"There are so many consolations."

LOVE LETTER TO THE IMF

I live in a land of harlequins
and mermaids
bored by beauty,

where children high on glue
fall asleep in the street
and Christ floats above the hills.

I live in a land of tin rooftops
and tangled cables
pilfering light from the grid.

I don't need much:
a soccer game, a plate of beans,
five days in February.

Any *puta* on Copacabana
knows there's no such thing
as free trade.

If you want to talk
about life and debt,
I sell lottery tickets by the docks
where the big ships come in,
their bellies full of riot gear
and powdered milk.

ENTER THE DRAGON

after Bruce Lee

Not thinking, not dreaming;
moving like water.
The pliable reed doesn't snap.

No actor but action.
Enter the dragon.
Enter the mockingbird's throat.

Liking is pointless.
Disliking is pointless.
Respond as an echo;
master each sequence
until you achieve no technique.

Not grasping, not sticking.
When still, be a mirror.
Let go of your structured despair.

The problem's the answer.
Enter the dragon.
Enter the mockingbird's throat.

MACHINE

We are the fuel. The foul. The unclean.
It's labor day in the neighborhood;
Prince Tuesday wants to be a machine.

Maybe she's bored with it, maybe it's Maybelline.
It is vague but understood.
We are the flu. The shroud. The vaccine.

Masters of the Flying Guillotine.
I touch the earth less than I should.
Prince pirouettes on the wrecking machine.

M&Ms and M-16s:
which are a universal good?
We are the futile. The plowed. The routine.

The bees won't survive the Anthropocene.
A Banana stands where some pines once stood.
Rinse my little-read love machine;

it's a dirge on the verge of being obscene.
I found my cell in a dark wood.
We are the feud. The fraud. The foreseen.
INSTAMAZOMBITCHARLIESHEEN

SAFFRON

Later, when she went online,
a pop-up ad opened; strange,
she thought, an ad for saffron,
I was just... but how?..., saffron,
brillo of blood, tangled threads
of wine, and at a good price.
You see, her smart phone had been
eavesdropping on our breakfast,
awake, alert and attuned,
scanning spoken syllables;
in some ways ignorant, but
in some ways terrifying,
the small machine's access to
unlimited resources,
vast fields of sleepy saffron,
warehouses of boxed spices.
Spied upon, we didn't need
to stress: we're not terrorists
except in the usual,
boring, American way:
buying things, paying taxes,
earning miles and free shipping.
She had said of the pudding:
*There's a hint of rose water
and saffron.* Something's turned on
and listening, even better,
even worse, remembering,
which is a way of saving
and a way of being saved.
Something understands what you
are saying but never all
you are saying; not even
you understand all you say.
The taut, invisible web
in which we are suspended
feels our next movement but fails

to comprehend the slight ache
of a lazy fricative,
the delicate misery
of a luxurious spice.
The corms were planted by hands
of children, purple flowers
plucked by hands of children, too,
somewhere in the arid fields
of Persia. Then each saffron
stigma was snapped, no snipped, piled
and dried and packed and loaded
onto ships on slow journeys
to my local market's shelves
or directly to my door.
All this you learn on YouTube.
But something's always listening:
a machine tucked in your purse,
or bright, enormous machines
ranging the abyss of space,
or, beneath the stove, a mouse
with every right to steal crumbs.
Something is listening in me,
something alive that responds
to the cicada's long cry,
the muted constant whirring
of my laptop, sleeping not,
hushing trains of summer rain,
the ceiling fan's strange stillness;
and I move through endless tides
of sound without me knowing,
but something in me responds.
I'm thinking about the thing
in me, near me, or with me
that listens to the deep song
of the nothing. I'm talking
about the soul and other
voice recognition systems.

479

Because I culled the grains of leisure.
Because I cooed at passing children.
Because the fields are setting.
Because I killed the horses.

Because I could not stop.
Because the grazing sun.
Because I'm such a tulle.
Because my gaze is centuries.

Because I labor then I chill.
Because the tippet's torn.
Because a swelling haste.
Because it's ringed with dew.

Because the chorus in the ground.
Because the corn is in my quiver.
Because I strove at school
but was scarcely visible to me.

Because I had been put away.
Because I pulled the knots of death.
Because I drew myself a roof
of immorality.

THE BORROWED CHAPEL

In huddled woods we wed,
robed in ribbonned light,
beneath the wild choir
of hermit thrushes thronging
swaying ladders of evergreen,
flanked by the drunken glow
of swollen fireflies
staining the breath of grasses
with lust-encrusted codes.
We were pollen-flecked and poised,
drinking the bright wine
of our parents' tears, inking
our names in the black brook,
the clear water's ledger,
the fir-knitted night
our borrowed chapel, the thrum
and whir of bees retreating
to muster in golden girdles,
cicadas shaking free
of their sundered shells and fern—
flocks burdened bending
with so much abandoned armor,
bullfrogs opening chasms
of song, banners of lichen
fastened to forgotten kindling,
our bodies at night's bidding,
our words whittled down
to an ancient hush harbored
in the green empire of moss.

BROWN PAPER BAG

A paper bag drifting across the sands:
the wind reveals itself to me.
As if loosened from an ancient sleep,
a seagull sings above the tides.

The wind reveals itself to me;
I know it only by what it touches:
a seagull sings above the tides.
I'm asking for just a little time;

I know it only by what it touches:
the sea catches fire then turns to ash.
I'm asking for just a little time
to bend like a reed beneath the moon.

The sea catches fire then turns to ash.
Naked flesh knows what it needs
to bend like a reed beneath the moon.
There is nothing in the world that does not move.

Naked flesh knows what it needs.
The stone is the quietest of birds.
There is nothing in the world that does not move.
Only God is alone.

The stone is the quietest of birds.
A wave follows another wave;
only God is alone.
The waking body is my door.

A wave follows another wave;
it swells to crest in a shivering cloud.
The waking body is my door.
The seagull leaves but takes no road;

it swells to crest in a shivering cloud.
It's the patient eye that understands.
The seagull leaves but takes no road;
I want to lift myself that way.

It's the patient eye that understands
a paper bag drifting across the sands.
I want to lift myself that way,
as if loosened from an ancient sleep.

THE NIGHT I TURNED TO WATER

The night I turned to water
I wandered fields of fences;
water's the one thing
a net can never hold.

I watched my body unfold.

The night I turned to water
I could tear without being torn.
I was naked at last, a naked
that makes no sense to a man.

My only shirt was the moon.

The night I turned to water
I learned nothing keeps still,
not even the heaviest stones.
I moved in a world without words,

kissed by nodding weeds.

The night I turned to water
the lights of planes and the swell
of stars fell in me,
but I couldn't dream of them.

I traveled the road of the stem.

The night I turned to water
I walked into shut seeds
of sweat and fleeting dew
and a body's slender pores.

I tested the tightest doors.

The night I turned to water
I sprayed the crested terns
with salt. The wind was my sister,
and she danced on the sheets of the tide.

I was neither groom nor bride.

The night I turned to water
I slipped the knot of the state.
A skimmer's wing was my flag,
my song the brutal waves.

I was never asked to be brave.

The night I turned to water
I rained on wrecked refugees
held in unbroken sleep,
and yet I couldn't weep.

I had become the weeping.

MOURNING DOVE'S METER

I thought it was a *morning dove*
because in the morning I would wake
to the bird's sullen spondee.

I thought the phrase was
to *wet*, not *whet*,
the appetite.

I heard of armies *razing*
ancient city walls
and believed
they were *raising* those walls—
ominous,
that homonym.
So it wasn't a miracle of creation
but one of destruction,
which, looking back now,
hardly seems a wonder at all.

In my inaccuracies,
I was not entirely inaccurate.
The mourning dove
is not mourning;
it's a song we've translated
in error.

But to bring the dove into my work,
how shall I warble myself?

I'll be a mockingbird
in my dictionary perched
and with the mourning dove's meter
sing back:

dawn's dooms,

                    dew-

                    strewn

those bitches blew

                    plumed

                    flutes

my tippet, tulle

                    a fool's

                    ruse

if bright spool,

                    rude

                    loom

a wild croon

                    my brute

                    fuse

CHILD

The quiet of a child
is a not having
that is yes.

It takes time to see,
and what you see
is always over there.

It takes time to understand,
and what you understand
is only wisdom.

Where is the carousel
of startled horses?

A child
within the child;
neither visible to the other.

Being young came and went
as though it had nothing to do with you.

POEM FOR MICHAEL K.

Toward what dim city are you walking?
Are there signs that mark the roads you took?
I remember the married women
who traded happiness for your kisses.
Where were the women when
your bed was a shipwreck?
There's a little room left on your pillow for laughter.
I never wanted to write this letter.
Wait for me beneath the maple,
beneath your flag of fire.
An awful flower unfolded in the night.
A fish is caught in nets of wrinkled water.
Nothing is alive that is not waking.
Nothing is alive that does not wander.
I'm close to the pit of the plum.
Which of us now is more alone?
Michael, this poem is the rose in my throat.
Toward what dim city are you walking?
Have all the roads vanished but one?

I TURNED MY BACK ON WORDS

I turned my back on words
to speak another way
but when I spoke stones
I couldn't penetrate them

so I learned to speak water
but once I mastered it I quickly desisted
because I began to lose myself
in what I was saying

then I studied wind
the discourse of air
but spoke with such clarity
I could keep nothing secret

finally I tended fire
to make my tongue a flame
but feared the simplest things I said
would turn me into ash

PRAYER TO SAN LAZARO DE MONSANTO

Bless my garden.
Bless my lawn.
Bless the long spears of onion grass.
Bless the starred orbs of dandelion.
Bless me, San Lazaro de Monsanto.

Bless the exiled monarch.
Bless the mason bee.
Bless the milkweed.
Bless the weeds of my mind.
Intercede on my behalf, Saint Bayer.

Bless my throat.
Bless my brow with a rancid kiss.
Bless my baby's slender spine.
Bless the mother's milk.
Undress our nights of crickets.
Comb the pearls from the earth.

DREAMING IN PORTUGUESE

In Portuguese, one says:
Sonhei com você.
In English, it's the same as saying,
"I dreamed of you."
It's the same and not the same,
because in Portuguese
one is actually saying,
"I dreamed with you"—
but that's not what is meant,
or perhaps it is,
or perhaps what is meant is never
what one says.

I dreamed with you.
So there are two kinds of dreaming.
Or perhaps there is one dreaming
but two ways to dream
of dreaming.

I'm thinking of "of,"
I'm struggling with "with,"
and my mind wonders
at the subtle sutures of a language,
the sorcery in the stitch
that hems my thought.

BLADE

the body's night
opened starless
throat unbuttoned
what touches my body
is by my body
touched the hand
that pruned a tumor's
tumid vine
fingered the compass
deep in the marrow
tilled my blood
stitched tomorrow
across my brow
broke me to mend me
splayed my face
in sprays of poppies
all my pockets
emptied turned
inside out
who wandered the maze
of my making wielded
the blade that blessed me
in blood that dressed me
myself my guest
my life a glade
of borrowed light
and tenacious dreaming
while flesh unfolded
in wild unfastening
before a cure
of cruelest weaving
from the first oblivion
we arrive here wounded
welcomed by hunger
from the pulsing knot
wrenched free

MARIO QUINTANA:
selected poems translated by Johnny Lorenz

PARÁBOLA?

Os espelhos partidos têm muito mais luas.

TEXTO & PRETEXTO

O tema é um ponto de partida para um poema e não um ponto de chegada, da mesma forma que a bem-amada é um pretexto para o amor.

DO SONHO

Sonhar é acordar-se para dentro.

EVOLUÇÃO

O que me impressiona, à vista de um macaco, não é que ele tenha sido nosso passado: é este pressentimento de que ele venha a ser o nosso futuro.

PARABLE?

There are many more moons in broken mirrors.

TEXT & PRETEXT

The theme is a point of departure for a poem and not a destination, in the same way that the beloved is a pretext for loving.

OF DREAMS

To dream is to wake within.

EVOLUTION

What strikes me at the sight of a monkey is not that he's been our past: it's this feeling he'll be our future.

TRISTEZA DE ESCREVER

Cada palavra é uma borboleta morta espetada na página:
Por isso a palavra escrita é sempre triste...

OS INTERMEDIÁRIOS

Não me ajeito com os padres, os críticos e os canudinhos de refresco... Não há nada que substitua o sabor da comunicação direta.

DA SAUDADE

A saudade que dói mais fundo – e irremediavelmente – é a saudade que temos de nós.

CIRCO

A verdade é que os bichos, quando imitam pessoas, perdem toda a dignidade.

SADNESS OF WRITING

Each word is a dead butterfly pinned to the page:
That's why the written word is always sad...

THE INTERMEDIARIES

I can't deal with priests, critics or drinking straws... Nothing substitutes for the taste of direct communication.

OF LONGING

The longing that hurts most deeply – and is without remedy – is the longing we feel for ourselves.

CIRCUS

The truth is that animals, when they imitate people, lose all their dignity.

TEMPO

Coisa que acaba de deixar a querida leitora um pouco mais velha ao chegar ao fim desta linha.

UM POUCO DE GEOMETRIA

A curva é o caminho mais agradável entre dois pontos.

FÉ

Uma das coisas que não consigo absolutamente compreender são os que se convertem a outras religiões. Para que mudar de dúvidas?

DA INFINITA SOLIDÃO

Mas só Deus – que é único, que não tem par – poderia dizer o que é a solidão.

TIME

What has just left our dear reader a little older upon arriving at the end of this line.

A LITTLE GEOMETRY

The curve is the most pleasing distance between two points.

FAITH

I absolutely cannot comprehend people who convert to other religions. Why exchange your old doubts for new ones?

OF INFINITE SOLITUDE

But only God – who is singular, who has no equal – could say what solitude is.

ARS LONGA

Um poema só termina por acidente de publicação ou de morte do autor.

PROSÓDIA

As folhas enchem de ff as vogais do vento.

O TEMPO

O tempo é a insônia da eternidade.

URBANÍSTICA

Como seriam belas as estátuas eqüestres se constassem apenas dos cavalos!

ARS LONGA

A poem is finished only by accident: publication, or the death of the poet.

PROSODY

The shaking leaves fill with *sh* the vowels of the wind.

TIME

Time is the insomnia of eternity.

URBANISTIC

How beautiful the equestrian statues would be if they consisted only of horses!

O POEMA

Um poema como um gole dágua bebido no escuro.
Como um pobre animal palpitando ferido.
Como pequenina moeda de prata perdida para sempre na floresta noturna.
Um poema sem outra angústia que a sua misteriosa condição de poema.
Triste.
Solitário.
Único.
Ferido de mortal beleza.

EXAME DE INCONSCIÊNCIA

Há noites em que não posso dormir de remorsos por tudo o que deixei de cometer...

E DAÍ?

Falam muito no Sono Eterno. Sempre falaram, aliás... E daí?
Daí, só uma coisa me impressiona, e muito: a ameaça de uma Insônia Eterna.

O HUMILDE TESOURO

Ah, nem queiras saber... A vida é preciosa como um pão roubado!

THE POEM

A poem like a gulp of water swallowed in the dark.
Like a poor animal trembling wounded.
Like a small silver coin lost forever in the nocturnal woods.
A poem free from any anguish save its own mysterious condition.
Sad.
Solitary.
Singular.
Wounded by mortal beauty.

SELF-EXAMINATION

There are nights I stay awake with regret for all the sins I did not commit…

SO?

They talk a lot about the Eternal Sleep. In fact, they've always talked about it… and so?
So then, just one thing disturbs me, and disturbs me a lot: the threat of an Eternal Insomnia.

HUMBLE TREASURE

Ah, you don't even want to know… Life is precious like stolen bread!

SONHO DE UMA NOITE DE VERÃO

*Uma procissão de espantalhos,
pela miséria colorida,
pelos atalhos
vinha:
pediam vida, queriam vida!
E as suas caras eram trágicas
porque tinham todas a mesma expressão
– que era o mesmo que não terem nenhuma expressão.
E tão insuportável era aquela cara única
que a polícia atirou em cima deles bombas de gás hilariante.
Nenhum espantalho riu.
A procissão continuou,
a procissão está agora em plena Estrada Real
enquanto
pelos atalhos
por toda a parte
por cima dos gramados
por cima dos corpos atropelados
os automóveis fogem como baratas.*

O SUPREMO CASTIGO

Em todos os aeródromos, em todos os estádios, no ponto principal de todas as metrópoles, existe – quem é que não viu? – aquele cartaz...

De modo que, se esta civilização desaparecer e seus dispersos e bárbaros sobreviventes tiverem de recomeçar tudo desde o princípio – até que um dia também tenham os seus próprios arqueólogos – estes hão de sempre encontrar, nos mais diversos pontos do mundo inteiro, aquela mesma palavra.

E pensarão eles que Coca-Cola era o nome do nosso Deus!

A MIDSUMMER NIGHT'S DREAM

A procession of scarecrows,
colored by misery,
down the side streets
it came:
they asked for life; they wanted to live!
And their faces were tragic
because they all had the same expression
– which is the same as having no expression at all.
And so intolerable was that one face
that the police threw bombs of laughing gas at them.
Not a single scarecrow laughed.
The procession continued;
now it's coming down the Estrada Real,
while
down the side streets
all around
over lawns
over trampled bodies
the automobiles flee like roaches.

SUPREME PUNISHMENT

Around all the airports, in all the stadiums, at the center of every metropolis, you will find – who hasn't seen it? – that billboard…

Such that if this civilization were to disappear, and if its dispersed, barbarous survivors had to start everything all over again – and if one day they should even have their own archaeologists – they'd encounter, again and again, in the most far-flung places on earth, that same word.

And they'll think that Coca-Cola was the name of our God!

SE O POETA FALAR NUM GATO

Se o poeta falar num gato, numa flor,
num vento que anda por descampados e desvios
e nunca chegou à cidade...
se falar numa esquina mal e mal iluminada...
numa antiga sacada... num jogo de dominó...
se falar naqueles obedientes soldadinhos de chumbo
            que morriam de verdade...
se falar na mão decepada no meio de uma escada
           de caracol...
Se não falar em nada
e disser simplesmente tralalá... Que importa?
Todos os poemas são de amor!

A LUA DE BABILÔNIA

Numa esquina do Labirinto
às vezes
avista-se a Lua.
"Não! como é possível uma lua subterrânea?"

(Mas cada um diz baixinho:
Deus te abençoe, visão...)

O ESPECTADOR

Olhar a televisão
Sem prestar atenção,
Ver apenas figuras a moverem-se na tela
E só assim talvez terei alguma compreensão
Da nossa vida e do sentido dela...

IF THE POET WERE TO SPEAK OF A CAT

If the poet were to speak of a cat, of a flower,
of a wind that travels over fields and byways
without ever reaching the city...
if the poet were to speak of a bad street corner badly lit...
of an old balcony... of a game of dominos...
if the poet were to speak of those obedient tin soldiers
      that really died...
if the poet were to speak of the severed hand in the middle
      of a spiral staircase...
If the poet were to speak of nothing at all
but simply said tra-la-la... What does it matter?
Every poem is a love poem!

THE MOON OF BABYLON

In a corner of the Labyrinth
sometimes
the moon appears.
"No! How could there be a subterranean moon?"

(But each of us whispers:
God bless you, vision...)

THE SPECTATOR

Watching television
Without paying attention,
Just seeing figures move on the screen —
Maybe that's how I'll have some comprehension
Of what our lives might mean.

O UMBIGO

O teu querido umbiguinho,
Doce ninho do meu beijo
Capital do meu Desejo,
Em suas dobras misteriosas,
Ouço a voz da natureza
Num eco doce e profundo,
Não só o centro de um corpo,
Também o centro do mundo!

POEMINHO DO CONTRA

Todos esses que aí estão
Atravancando o meu caminho,
Eles passarão...
Eu passarinho!

DA REALIDADE

O sumo bem só no ideal perdura...
Ah! quanta vez a vida nos revela
Que "a saudade da amada criatura"
É bem melhor do que a presença dela...

BELLY BUTTON

Your dear belly button,
Capital of my Desire,
Sweet nest of kisses,
There, in its echoing gyre,
I hear nature's voice,
Where your skin's mysteriously curled.
It's not the center of a body
But the center of the world.

LITTLE PROTEST POEM   (version 1)

These people are all alike;
They stymie everything.
Some day they'll take a hike...
But I take wing!

LITTLE PROTEST POEM   (version 2)

These hindering hordes, this teeming mass,
They're getting under my skin.
All of them in time will pass...
I will passerine!

OF REALITY

Perfection's only an ideal...
How often you discover
The longing you feel is better than
The company of your lover...

DO ESPETÁCULO DESTA VIDA

Impossível será que melhor vida exista,
Enquanto o mundo assim se distribuir:
No palco a Estupidez, para ser vista,
E a Inteligência na platéia, a rir...

DA DISCRIÇÃO

Não te abras com teu amigo
Que ele um outro amigo tem.
E o amigo de teu amigo
Possui amigos também...

DAS UTOPIAS

Se as coisas são inatingíveis... ora!
Não é motivo para não querê-las...
Que tristes os caminhos, se não fora
A presença distante das estrelas!

DA PAZ INTERIOR

O sossego interior, se queres atingi-lo,
Não deixes coisa alguma incompleta ou adiada.
Não há nada que dê um sono mais tranqüilo
Que uma vingança bem executada...

OF THE SPECTACLE THAT IS LIFE

The world, I fear, won't change a bit,
It's the same in every age:
Intellect laughs in the mezzanine
While Stupidity takes the stage...

OF DISCRETION

Don't open up to your friend
If you have a secret to tell,
For your friend, too, has a friend
Who likely has friends as well...

OF UTOPIAS

Some dreams we can't achieve,
Try as we might,
But how sad the roads we walk if not
For distant stars at night!

OF INNER PEACE

If you're seeking inner peace,
Then finish every chore;
Nothing gives a good night's sleep
Like settling a score...

DA VERGONHA

Ora, o que sentes é puro
Receio de seres visto.
Não, vergonha não é isto:
Vergonha é a que tens no escuro...

DA INQUIETA ESPERANÇA

Bem sabes Tu, Senhor, que o bem melhor é aquele
Que não passa, talvez, de um desejo ilusório.
Nunca me dês o Céu... quero é sonhar com ele
Na inquietação feliz do Purgatório...

IV

Minha rua está cheia de pregões.
Parece que estou vendo com os ouvidos:
"Couves! Abacaxis! Cáquis! Melões!"
Eu vou sair pro Carnaval dos ruídos,

Mas vem, Anjo da Guarda... Por que pões
Horrorizado as mãos em teus ouvidos?
Anda: escutemos esses palavrões
Que trocam dois gavroches atrevidos!

Pra que viver assim num outro plano?
Entremos no bulício quotidiano...
O ritmo da rua nos convida.

Vem! Vamos cair na multidão!
Não é poesia socialista... Não,
Meu pobre Anjo... É... simplesmente... a Vida!...

OF SHAME

But what you're feeling isn't shame;
You're a little bit off the mark.
You're just afraid of being seen;
Shame is what you feel in the dark...

OF RESTLESS HOPE

Nothing's so dear as desire, Lord.
Don't give me Heaven's glory.
Let me dream of it in sweet unrest;
Just give me Purgatory...

IV

I hear the delights the vendors are selling;
It's as though I could somehow see with my ears:
"Cabbage! Pineapples! Persimmons! Melons!"
But my guardian angel covers his ears.

Why not join this carnival of noise?
Poor angel, your attitude is strange;
Come listen to the foul-mouthed boys...
What curses these two Gavroches exchange!

Why live your life on some other plane?
Join the bustle, don't complain...
The rhythm of the street invites us.

Angel, you must change your mood!
It's not socialist poetry, it's the multitude...
Life itself is what delights us!...

V

Eu nada entendo da questão social.
Eu faço parte dela, simplesmente...
E sei apenas do meu próprio mal,
Que não é bem o mal de toda a gente,

Nem é deste Planeta... Por sinal
Que o mundo se lhe mostra indiferente!
E o meu Anjo da Guarda, ele somente,
É quem lê os meus versos afinal...

E enquanto o mundo em torno se esbarronda,
Vivo regendo estranhas contradanças
No meu vago País de Trebizonda...

Entre os Loucos, os Mortos e as Crianças,
É lá que eu canto, numa eterna ronda,
Nossos comuns desejos e esperanças!...

VI

Na minha rua há um menininho doente.
Enquanto os outros partem para a escola,
Junto à janela, sonhadoramente,
Ele ouve o sapateiro bater sola.

Ouve também o carpinteiro, em frente,
Que uma canção napolitana engrola.
E pouco a pouco, gradativamente,
O sofrimento que ele tem se evola...

Mas nesta rua há um operário triste:
Não canta nada na manhã sonora
E o menino nem sonha que ele existe.

Ele trabalha silenciosamente...
E está compondo este soneto agora,
Pra alminha boa do menino doente...

V

What does the "social question" mean?
I am a part of it, that's plain.
I know the things that cause me pain
Are not the same for every man.

My pain is alien; I can tell
By the indifference of the world.
Who will read my rhyming words?
No one but my guardian angel.

So while this planet comes undone,
I'll conduct a strange quadrille
In Trebizond, my vague nation,

And never will the dance be still.
Among the mad and dead and young,
I sing our common aspiration!...

VI

The boy who lives nearby is ill;
The other children leave for school.
As the cobbler pounds away at soles,
The sick boy listens by the sill.

He also listens to the song
A carpenter mumbles happily,
An ancient tune from Napoli;
The young lad's pain does not last long.

But there's a worker who is sad;
He's singing not a single note.
The boy knows nothing of this neighbor

Who quietly goes about his labor,
Writing this sonnet all the while
For the good soul of a sick child...

XVII

Da vez primeira em que me assassinaram
Perdi um jeito de sorrir que eu tinha...
Depois, de cada vez que me mataram,
Foram levando qualquer coisa minha...

E hoje, dos meus cadáveres, eu sou
O mais desnudo, o que não tem mais nada...
Arde um toco de vela, amarelada...
Como o único bem que me ficou!

Vinde, corvos, chacais, ladrões da estrada!
Ah! desta mão, avaramente adunca,
Ninguém há de arrancar-me a luz sagrada!

Aves da Noite! Asas do Horror! Voejai!
Que a luz, trêmula e triste como um ai,
A luz do morto não se apaga nunca!

XXIII

Cidadezinha cheia de graça...
Tão pequenina que até causa dó!
Com seus burricos a pastar na praça...
Sua igrejinha de uma torre só...

Nuvens que venham, nuvens e asas,
Não param nunca nem um segundo...
E fica a torre, sobre as velhas casas,
Fica cismando como é vasto o mundo!...

Eu que de longe venho perdido,
Sem pouso fixo (a triste sina!)
Ah, quem me dera ter lá nascido!

Lá toda a vida poder morar!
Cidadezinha... Tão pequenina
Que toda cabe num só olhar...

XVII

The first time that they murdered me,
I lost the smile that's mine alone.
Each time they killed me afterward,
They took another thing I owned…

Of my cadavers, I'm the one
Laid most bare and most bereft.
A bit of candle, dimly lit…
It's all that I have left.

Come now, jackals, crooks and crows!
My fingers, gnarled, will not let go;
No one steals this sacred light.

Beat your wings, birds of night!
It's as sad and trembling as a sigh,
But the light of the dead can never die!

XXIII

I even pity this little town.
Just look how small it is, how fair –
Mules left grazing in the square,
The church with just one lonely tower.

Never pausing in the wind,
The birds pass by, as do the clouds.
The tower keeps watch above old houses
And wonders on this endless world.

I keep moving on, with no address;
It's what fate has decided for me, I guess.
But I'd love to call this place my home!

I could live my life in a town this size,
A town so small that I can hold
It all inside my eyes.

O MAPA

Olho o mapa da cidade
Como quem examinasse
A anatomia de um corpo...

(É nem que fosse o meu corpo!)

Sinto uma dor infinita
Das ruas de Porto Alegre
Onde jamais passarei...

Há tanta esquina esquisita,
Tanta nuança de paredes,
Há tanta moça bonita
Nas ruas que não andei
(E há uma rua encantada
Que nem em sonhos sonhei...)

Quando eu for, um dia desses,
Poeira ou folha levada
No vento da madrugada,
Serei um pouco do nada
Invisível, delicioso

Que faz com que o teu ar
Pareça mais um olhar,
Suave mistério amoroso,
Cidade de meu andar
(Deste já tão longo andar!)

E talvez de meu repouso...

THE MAP

I look at the map of the city
Like someone studying
The anatomy of a body...

(It could be my own body.)

I feel an endless ache
For the streets of Porto Alegre
That I will never take.

There are so many curious turns,
So many nuances of walls,
So many beautiful girls
In the streets I never walked
(And there's a street I would love
That even in dreams I've not dreamt of...)

When I turn to dust,
One of these days, or leaf
Lifted by the breeze
At dawn, I'll be a bit
Of that delicious nothing
No one sees but is there

And makes the very air
Seem somehow to gaze.
Delicate, amorous mystery,
City that I wander
(Where even now I lumber)

City, perhaps, of my slumber...

CARTA

Meu caro poeta,

  Por um lado foi bom que me tivesses pedido resposta urgente, senão eu jamais escreveria sobre o assunto desta, pois não possuo o dom discursivo e expositivo, vindo daí a dificuldade que sempre tive de escrever em prosa. A prosa não tem margens, nunca se sabe quando, como e onde parar. O poema, não; descreve uma parábola traçada pelo próprio impulso (ritmo); é que nem um grito. Todo poema é, para mim, uma interjeição ampliada; algo de instintivo, carregado de emoção. Com isso não quero dizer que o poema seja uma descarga emotiva, como o faziam os românticos. Deve, sim, trazer uma carga emocional, uma espécie de radioatividade, cuja duração só o tempo o dirá. Por isso há versos de Camões que nos abalam tanto até hoje e há versos de hoje que os pósteros lerão com aquela cara com que lemos os de Filinto Elísio. Aliás, a posteridade é muito comprida: me dá sono. Escrever com o olho na posteridade é tão absurdo como escreveres para os súditos de Ramsés II, ou para o próprio Ramsés, se fores palaciano. Quanto a escrever para os contemporâneos, está muito bem, mas como é que vais saber quem são os teus contemporâneos? A única contemporaneidade que existe é a da contingência política e social, porque estamos mergulhados nela, mas isto compete melhor aos discursivos e expositivos, aos oradores e catedráticos. Que sobra então para a poesia? – perguntarás. E eu te respondo que sobras tu. Achas pouco? Não me refiro à tua pessoa, refiro-me ao teu eu, que transcende os teus limites pessoais, mergulhando no humano. O Profeta diz a todos: "eu vos trago a Verdade", enquanto o poeta, mais humildemente, limita-se a dizer a cada um: "eu te trago a minha verdade". E o poeta, quanto mais individual, mais universal, pois cada homem, qualquer que seja o condicionamento do meio e da época, só vem a compreender e amar o que é essencialmente humano. Embora, eu que o diga, seja tão difícil ser assim autêntico. Às vezes assalta-me o terror de que todos os meus poemas sejam apócrifos!

  Meu poeta, se estas linhas estão te aborrecendo é porque és poeta mesmo. Modéstia à parte, as digressões sobre poesia sempre me causaram tédio e perplexidade. A culpa é tua, que me pediste conselho e me colocas na insustentável situação em que me vejo quando essas meninas dos colégios vêm (por inocência ou maldade dos professores) fazer pesquisas com perguntas assim: "O que é poesia? Por que se tornou poeta? Como escreve os seus poemas?" A poesia é dessas coisas que a gente faz mas não diz.

CARTA

My dear poet,

On the one hand, it's good that you've asked me for a quick reply, or else I never would have written on this topic, since I don't possess discursive or expository ability, which explains the difficulty I've always had in writing prose. Prose has no margins; one never knows when, how or where to stop. The poem is different; it follows a parabola traced by its own impulse (rhythm); it's like a cry. Every poem is, to me, an amplified interjection; something instinctive and charged with emotion. By this, I don't mean to say that the poem should be an emotional release, in the manner of the Romantics. It should, yes, have an emotional charge, a kind of radioactivity whose duration lasts only time will tell how long. For this reason there are verses by Camões that move us even today, and there are verses written today that future readers will read with the same face we make when reading Filinto Elísio. Besides, posterity is very long: it makes me sleepy. To write with your eye fixed on posterity is as absurd as writing for the subjects of Ramses II, or for Ramses himself, should you be a court poet. As for writing for your contemporaries, that's fine, but how will you know who your contemporaries are? The only contemporaneity that exists is that of political and social contingency, because we are immersed in it, but that's better left to those who give speeches and explanations, the orators and professors. You will ask: What's left, then, for poetry? And I respond: what's left is you. Do you think that's not enough? I am not referring to your person but rather to the "I" that transcends your personal limits and immerses itself in all that is human. The Prophet says to everyone: "I bring ye the Truth," while the poet, more modestly, limits himself to saying to each of us: "I bring you my truth." And for the poet, the more individual he is, the more universal, for each man, whatever the circumstance of milieu or epoch, only comes to comprehend and love that which is essentially human. However, let me say, it's difficult to be authentic in this way. I am sometimes assaulted by the terrifying idea that all my poems are apocryphal.

My poet, if these lines bore you, it's because you really are a poet. Modesty aside, digressions about poetry are always tedious

A poesia é um fato consumado, não se discute; perguntas-me, no entanto, que orientação de trabalho seguir e que poetas deves ler. Eu tinha vontade de ser um grande poeta para te dizer como é que eles fazem. Só te posso dizer o que eu faço. Não sei como vem um poema. Às vezes uma palavra, uma frase ouvida, uma repentina imagem que me ocorre em qualquer parte, nas ocasiões mais insólitas. A esta imagem respondem outras. Por vezes uma rima até ajuda, com o inesperado da sua associação. (Em vez de associações de idéias, associações de imagens; creio ter sido esta a verdadeira conquista da poesia moderna.) Não lhes oponho trancas nem barreiras. Vai tudo para o papel. Guardo o papel, até que um dia o releio, já esquecido de tudo (a falta de memória é uma bênção nestes casos). Vem logo o trabalho de corte, pois noto logo o que estava demais ou o que era falso. Coisas que pareciam tão bonitinhas, mas que eram puro enfeite, coisas que eram puro desenvolvimento lógico (um poema não é um teorema) tudo isso eu deito abaixo, até ficar o essencial, isto é, o poema. Um poema tanto mais belo é quanto mais parecido for com um cavalo. Por não ter nada de mais nem nada de menos é que o cavalo é o mais belo ser da Criação.

Como vês, para isso é preciso uma luta constante. A minha está durando a vida inteira. O desfecho é sempre incerto. Sinto-me capaz de fazer um poema tão bom ou tão ruinzinho como aos 17 anos. Há na Bíblia uma passagem que não sei que sentido lhe darão os teólogos; é quando Jacob entra em luta com um anjo e lhe diz: "Eu não te largarei até que me abençoes". Pois bem, haverá coisa melhor para indicar a luta do poeta com o poema? Não me perguntes, porém, a técnica dessa luta sagrada ou sacrílega. Cada poeta tem de descobrir, lutando, os seus próprios recursos. Só te digo que deves desconfiar dos truques da moda, que, quando muito, podem enganar o público e trazer-te uma efêmera popularidade.

Em todo caso, bem sabes que existe a métrica. Eu tive a vantagem de nascer numa época em que só se podia poetar dentro dos moldes clássicos. Era preciso ajustar as palavras naqueles moldes, obedecer àquelas rimas. Uma bela ginástica, meu poeta, que muitos de hoje acham ingenuamente desnecessária. Mas, da mesma forma que a gente primeiro aprendia nos cadernos de caligrafia para depois, com o tempo, adquirir uma letra própria, espelho grafológico da sua individualidade, eu na verdade te digo que só tem capacidade e moral para criar um ritmo livre quem for capaz de escrever um soneto clássico. Verás com o tempo que cada poema, aliás, impõe a sua forma; uns, as canções, já vêm dançando, com as rimas de mãos dadas, outros, os dionisíacos (ou histriônicos, como queiras) até parecem aqualoucos. E um conselho, afinal: não cortes demais (um poema não é

and perplexing to me. The blame is entirely yours, since you asked me for advice and put me in the unbearable situation in which I find myself when schoolgirls (due to their innocence or their teachers' wickedness) conduct research by asking me questions such as: "What is poetry? Why did you become a poet? How do you write your poems?" Poetry is one of those things we do but do not talk about.

Poetry is a consummated fact, not to be discussed; you ask me, meanwhile, for guidance and for the names of poets you should read. I would've liked to have been a great poet in order to tell you what the great poets do. I can only tell you what I do. I don't know how a poem arrives. Sometimes it's a word, a sentence heard, a sudden image that occurs to me somewhere in the most unusual moments. And other images respond to that image. Sometimes a rhyme even helps, a relationship that produces the unexpected. (Instead of associations of ideas, associations of images; I believe this is the real triumph of modern poetry.) Everything goes down on paper, without hindrance or obstacle. I put the paper away until the day I re-read it, after having forgotten everything (the lack of memory is a blessing in such cases). Soon afterwards comes the work of editing, for I soon become aware of what was exaggerated or false. Things that seemed so beautiful, but were pure adornment; things that were purely logical development (a poem is not a theorem); all of this I tear down until only the essential remains, which is the poem. The more beautiful a poem, the more it resembles a horse. The horse has nothing in excess, nor does it lack anything, and for that reason, in all of creation, nothing is more beautiful.

As you can see, a constant struggle is required. My struggle has lasted my entire life. The outcome is always uncertain. I feel capable of writing a poem as good or as bad as those I wrote when I was seventeen. There is a passage in the Bible, I don't know what meaning the theologians would give it, when Jacob wrestles with an angel and tells him: "I won't let go of you until you bless me." Well then, could there be anything better to explain the struggle between the poet and the poem? But don't ask me about the skills necessary for this holy, or sacrilegious, battle. In this battle, each poet has to discover his own resources. I'll only tell you to be suspicious of whatever tricks are in style, which, at most, might fool the public and give you an ephemeral popularity.

In any case, you know that meter exists. I had the advantage

um esquema); eu próprio que tanto te recomendei a contenção, às vezes me distendo, me largo num poema que lá vai seguindo com os seus detritos, como um rio de enchente, e que me faz bem, porque o espreguiçamento é também uma ginástica. Desculpa se tudo isso é uma coisa óbvia; mas para muitos, que tu conheces, ainda não é; mostra-lhes, pois, estas linhas.

Agora, que poetas deves ler? Simplesmente os poetas de que gostares e eles assim te ajudarão a compreender-te, em vez de tu a eles. São os únicos que te convêm, pois cada um só gosta de quem se parece consigo. Já escrevi, e repito: o que chamam de influência poética é apenas confluência. Já li poetas de renome universal e, mais grave ainda, de renome nacional, e que no entanto me deixaram indiferente. De quem a culpa? De ninguém. É que não eram da minha família.

Enfim, meu poeta, trabalhe, trabalhe em seus versos e em você mesmo e apareça-me daqui a vinte anos. Combinado?

of being born at a time when you could only write poems in classical forms. It was necessary to adapt one's language to those forms, to obey the rhymes. A beautiful kind of gymnastics, my poet, that many today naively think unnecessary. But in the same way that we traced our first letters to eventually acquire our own unique handwriting, the graphic mirror of individuality, I tell you truly that the only ones who have the ability and the confidence to write free verse are those who can write a classical sonnet. You will see with time, however, that any poem imposes its own form: some, the verses, already arrive dancing with their rhymes holding hands; others, the Dionysian poems (or histrionic, if you like) resemble *aqualoucos*, those high-diving clowns. A bit of advice, finally: don't cut too much (a poem is not a scheme); even I, who recommended to you restraint, sometimes stretch myself out; I let myself go in a poem that moves along with its detritus, like a flooded river, and it does me good, because stretching out is also a form of exercise. I apologize if all this seems obvious, but for many of those you know, it's not. Show them these lines, then.

Now, what poets should you read? Just the poets you'd like, and they'll help you understand yourself – instead of you understanding them. They are the only ones appropriate for you, since each person likes what resembles him. I wrote this once, but I'll repeat it: what they call poetic influence is only confluence. I have read poets of universal renown and, more serious yet, those of national renown, who nevertheless leave me feeling indifferent. Whose fault is that? Nobody's. They are simply not in my family.

Finally, my poet, work hard, work hard on your verses and on yourself and get back to me in twenty years. Agreed?

iii.

I begged for water;
they gave me wine.

POSTCARDS FROM THE LABYRINTH

I was banished from my mother's sleep.
Never again would I be held
by her small night,
without a pillow, unaware
of the need to be happy.

Other punishments awaited me.
I was taught to spell my name.

I was left alone with my body,
which never spoke to me.

I learned to count my days.

Money was given me
but never to keep.

I moved between the machines
that outnumber us.

I discovered wine:
every bottle a journal of twilight.

There are secret codes of grief.
I know the phone number
for the house I lived in as a child.

So many legs cross
the empty streets of my eyes.

Once, the A train drifted away from me
as I sat on the F.
I saw the face of a passenger
there on the other side,
and then I lost that face forever
in the labyrinth
beneath the labyrinth.

From an airplane,
I studied the smokestacks below,
the power plant and quiet offices lit
by late-night janitors.
I floated above a floor of stars.

Who will write an elegy for us,
the saddest of species?

How will the birds name themselves?

It was April,
and my love asked me:
Is this the last snow?
One never knows such things
until later. But I said yes
so I could miss the snow
as it was falling.

THE RUBBER-TAPPER'S WIFE

You leave a trail of wounded trees.

They wear the dim necklaces
you made with knives.

I sweep the veranda.
I soak the beans.
I hang the laundry,
our clean sheets spread wide
and without secrets.
I kill the kettle's song.

In the distance,
a big road slithers closer,
and I can't scare it away.

The rubber trees make a milk
no one can drink.

You never learned to read,
so I'll ask you to carry this paper
with you always
because only the things you can't explain
will protect you.

RAIN DIARY

No book can keep sheets of water.

The rain arrives without birthdays,
without an address.

When it rains in Miami,
fish wander into the street.
Doors are swollen shut.

New York City rain gets lost
between windows.

The rain in Vermont is afraid to die.

When is the rain ever silent?
When it's very far away.

In London the rain arrives
a century late,
bringing bad news
from the corners of the empire.

I heard a hushing rain
filling the streets of my sleep.

When I woke, the rain was falling,
slipping into windows
I had left open to the wind.

In Paris once,
I didn't know it was raining
until I tried to light a cigarette.

In Rio de Janeiro,
the rain pushes the poorest houses
down the hill
then goes around with kisses.

Must every book have a first and a last page?

The rain in San Juan
is the memory of rain.

A woman is walking,
rainwater cupped in her dark hands.
By the time she reaches me,
her hands will be empty.
There will be only the woman.

HORTÊNSIAS

Fora do alcance da minha memória,
a minha mãe é uma guria no sul do Brasil.
Ela não sabe meu nome.
Ela corre da carpintaria,
os dois dedos sangrados
e desunidos do seu pai
guardados nas mãos pequenas.

Quando as chuvas de inverno vêm
e o rio perde toda a disciplina,
o povo só pode olhar as águas vindo,
mas ninguém as estava chamando.
De uma cadeira levantada em cima de tijolos,
a minha mãe pode olhar para baixo as correntes
passando pela casa.
Qualquer coisa que flutua tenta escapar;
fotos, cartas de amor, as páginas de um calendário,
até uma jarra de álcool
em que dormem dois dedos
como peixes inocentes.

O verão vem, de onde não sei.
Nem de quando.
O corpo vivo é o relógio mais certo.
As hortênsias são quietas como sinos
quando ninguém os toca.

De noite, minha avó prepara
seu alarme de linhas de pesca
que correm do galinheiro até as latas enferrujadas
nas soleiras da casa.
Assim, ela pega ladrões,
mas, às vezes, é só o vento.

HYDRANGEAS

Beyond the reach of my memory,
my mother is a girl in the south of Brazil.
She doesn't know my name.
She runs out of the woodshop,
her father's two fingers,
bloody and severed,
cupped in her small hands.

When the winter rains arrive
and the river loses all discipline,
people can only watch the waters come,
but no one was calling.
From a chair lifted high on bricks,
my mother can look down at the currents
moving through the house.
Anything that floats tries to escape;
photos, love letters, pages of a calendar,
even a jar of alcohol
in which two fingers sleep
like innocent fish.

Summer arrives, I don't know from where.
Or from when.
The living body is the most precise clock.
The hydrangeas are quiet as bells
when no one touches them.

At night, my grandmother strings
her alarm of fishing wire
running from the chicken coop to rusty tin cans
on window sills.
That's how she catches thieves,
but, sometimes, it's just the wind.

THE VASE IN THE MAPLE

We brought the silver maple down.
With every storm a branch would fall,
and so we made them fall all at once
and winced at every thud.
When the shivering engines hushed,
the hired men told jokes in Spanish.
The stump remained, a wreck
behind the brownstone,
nestled against the chain-link fence.
I bent to trace the perfect rings,
a still ripple in the grain.
Then I touched something
that was not tree in the quiet breadth:
long ago a vase had lodged itself
within the trunk, or rather,
had been swallowed by the well of wood.
Its blue porcelain, half-exposed by rot
and webbed with faintest fractures,
had slipped deep into the fierce folds,
where the vase sleeps still.

THE WORD "QUINTESSENTIAL"

What is quintessential is not water;
it is not air or earth or even fire
but a fifth element,
the matter beyond matter,
the glassy skin of celestial spheres you cannot touch
making a music you cannot hear.
All our words are half asleep,
or something almost lost is sleeping in the word,
or the mind is sleepwalking
through the long corridors of our language.
Maybe the mind can never be awake enough
to fathom a word in its entirety;

it's like trying to cram the sea into your eyes,

it's like trying to listen to a song
all at once.

Perhaps the mind and the word
are two sleeps overlapping.
Blindness touches blindness,
and the miracle of meaning is that it happens precisely
from this mutual not-seeing,
because meaning must happen in error;
the mind is not visible to itself,
and any word pulses with the sap of an entire language.

My dream of God is a dictionary
that holds all the words
and all the words to come.

SÃO LEOPOLDO

The night leans its shoulder
against the wall
like a wounded elephant.

The people who live here,
you mean nothing to them.
I leave the front door open.

What passes by is mine
for a second.

Falar português é a minha maneira de te trair.

I once had reasons not to love you;
they are lost now,
like blackbirds at night.

I write you letters
because you no longer ask.
It's hard to finish an apple
or a piece of bread.

I discover the knives
only jealous lovers know.

On the corner,
someone's left a bottle of rum
for Exú.

LANDSCAPES WITHOUT POETRY

1.

The stone
is not a sparrow
cupped in your hands.

Sparrows on the ground
are not stones.

A woman waves hello,
or she waves goodbye;
do not confuse her hands
for sparrows.

I catch sparrows in my eyes,
but they mean nothing.

2.

A pelican loops
up and back
to pierce the blue
and pull from the tide
a bright mullet
writhing now
in the long beak.

No one sees
the swift kill,
not even the speaker
of the poem.

Long ago, the ocean
dreamed itself into being.

PRECISION

When Oxóssi hunts,
he hunts with a bow
and just one arrow.

Oxóssi never misses.

Unless you are a god,
you cannot inhabit perfection.
You can keep near.

In grade school,
I flirted with the girl who sat
behind the girl I had a crush on.

In my childhood prayers,
I said I was hardly sorry for my sins
instead of heartily.

The year I played soccer,
at the end of the season
I finally scored a goal;
it was against my own team.

I once played the lottery
and picked all 6 winning numbers
the week before they came in.

I was cruel
but only to the ones
who loved me.

The wrong road is still a road.

Success denies you the chance
to imagine what could have been.

YOUR HOUSE WITHOUT YOU

When you shut the door behind you
and walk away,
your house isn't empty.

Your pillow keeps nothing of your dreams.

Your windows have not forgotten you;
they do not remember you.

The door opens to you, yes,
but it would open to somebody else
if that person had the right key.

The quiet that fills the living room
is not quiet expectation
but simply quiet.

The coins beneath the sofa cushions are not lost.

All your life, you've been outside
the secret life of things.
Everything that is
is awake
without you.

THE BATH

> *Don't wash in a woman's bath-water, which for a time has a bitter vengeance in it.*
> —Hesiod

There's no hot water, she told me.
I couldn't pull myself from sleep,
so I moved into the dry warmth her body
had left beneath the blankets.

When I opened my eyes again,
she was sitting on a chair
naked in the middle of the room.
She held a kettle in her hand
and poured steaming water
into the folds of a white towel.

In one slow movement,
she wiped the damp cloth across
her right thigh, glistening now,
down to her ankle then wrung the towel
into the bucket at her feet.

Each time she poured the water
a brief mist lifted into the air,
and this quiet ablution of the flesh continued
as the soft light of morning
began to find her more and more.
She raised her left elbow
and moved the towel down
the underside of her arm
into the dark pit there and down further
to the heavy crescent of her breast.
It was a caress that belonged only to her.

And on it went,
no words between us,
but sometimes she looked at me looking,
sometimes she shivered
because she couldn't answer every part of her flesh,
the warm mouth of water
couldn't kiss her all at once,
and outside the winter seemed to deepen.

Then it was over,
almost a dream; she was dressed,
running late. I lifted the blinds
to watch her disappear
into the subway station across the street.

Alone now, I leaned over
the heavy bucket on the floor,
and with cupped hands,
like one of Gideon's men,
I brought the water to my tongue.

BLACKOUT IN SAPUCAIA DO SUL

Even the clock fell asleep.
The refrigerator stopped humming;
the chairs held their breath.
I didn't want to wake you, so this is my report.
I don't know why I stepped out into the doubled darkness.
A hidden chorus of frogs sang for the approaching rain.
I wandered beneath the hushed machinery of stars
that move above in ringing spheres.
The light of their bodies reaches farther
than the music they make.
Taxis waited with their headlights on,
drivers leaning their heads against bullet-proof glass.
A woman, her face lit by a candle,
sold coconut candy from her window.
A child on the corner had tucked himself
under newspaper, twitching
beneath the touch of mosquitoes.
A man hawking gold chains saluted me.
There was a girl in his lap like a guitar with no strings.
The high walls around us were decked
with broken bottles.
In the darkened streets, I came to understand
how one shadow is heavier than another,
how an absence traces the shape
of the body that is missing,
and how one silence differs from another
by what is not said.

THE V

The back of the boat
marked the beginning
of a widening V
written on water,
a letter that opened
and kept opening.
The distant ferry's wake penned
this majuscule on the surface
of my mind,
and between the two lines
of V, empty space
seemed to blossom.
The letter spread out
until it touched the nodding buoys
anchored to the blue,
lifted scattered swimmers up,
gently set them down,
nudged small fishing boats
and sent them softly rocking
in the shallows.
And though the V seemed
to dissipate in a fizzle of sea-spray,
I'm sure I saw the great figure
continue across sand
and narrow streets
until like a secret tide
it came to my window.

BABY RAT

There was nothing beautiful about it,
but I was too young to be certain of beauty.

Unblinking, unbreathing—
there was nothing there to save,
but I was too young
to decipher such grim signs.

So many things that kept completely still
had seemed to me alive:
I worried over solitary stones;
I mourned the shattered plate
and the stray button.

In the shade of a mangrove
by the quiet waters of a canal,
I waited for a dead baby rat
to wake in my hands.

I spoke to it gently
and stroked its brow.

I made a little bed for it
out of aluminum foil.

EDUCATION BY WINDOWS

after João Cabral de Melo Neto

No one teaches the waters
how to be naked,
and the way we learn
is by touching.

Sparrows taught me
leaving quickly.
The stone taught me
to sit beside the sparrow.

I was wandering a neighborhood
not my own, wondering at sunlit sills;
it isn't the way light moves
but how windows surrender their bodies.

I peered into an empty kitchen, just to see.
I was less respectable than a thief.

Nothing was there:
a breakfast table not yet cleared,
a loaf of bread, golden and broken
beside a sleeping knife,
napkins kissed, crumpled,
my shadow leaning on the wall.

My eyes belong to me
but not my visions.

I can't explain that day,
but everything matters to me now:
the lonely broom
and the progress of a snail.

SEBASTIAN

The most beautiful weapons
are the least effective:
sword, spear
and arrow.

You would not survive in the world I've inherited.
Some of the bullets miss, yes,
but there are many bullets,
and each one opens a fountain.

The time came when you stepped outside
the shadow of an empire.

You didn't weep
when your comrades lifted
their aching bows before you.

You didn't beg for mercy or pardon.
You didn't flinch when the first arrow
found your throat and kissed it.

Blessed be the traitors.

WRITING

You'll be reading these words
in the future, as though
you were being asked

to remember something,
and what you'll remember
isn't yours

but mine,
but somehow yours,
and when I'm writing,

I'll think of a word, perhaps
it's the word
that summons me,

and this encounter
happens not in space
because I can't tell you

if the word is before me
or next to me,
above or below me,

a bit behind me,
or maybe I am in the word
for a fleeting moment,

maybe the word is in me,
but then where does it go,
where does it wait when

we're apart from each other,
and how can I be certain of
what my words are trying to say,

when I'm not a credible witness
of myself,
because rarely,

if ever,
have I been able to see myself
since I am too close,

or too far away, and I can't explain
what the connection is
between my words and my life,

these words that seem to me
documents not of my experience
but of themselves,

except that I was here
when these words arrived,
I was the one who was writing

and the one being written,
and neither quite happening,
so I fail to understand me,

but failure is itself
a kind of knowing,
being wrong is my way,

error is my approach,
so why deny my voice
is itself a mistake,

or an illusion I prefer
to other illusions,
and taking for example

this very poem,
this voice I don't quite
"identify" with,

what if this
should be my voice,
when it's not really me,

like a man who envied others
their conviction, who wanted so badly
to be committed to something,

and the most important thing was not
to figure out what he believed
but simply to establish

what his beliefs might be and then
remain true to them,
so that after a certain point

there was no going back,
and just like that, what if my voice
is something I've pursued

out of some sense of loyalty
to myself,
when what is me

is partly
or even mostly
what I am not,

just as every single word
means what it says
and never says.

CARNAVAL

When I was a child,
wide awake in the waking world,
I would sit in the field
behind my father's house.
I kissed my folded knees
and the backs of my hands.
I bit into my arm and licked
thin sleeves of salt.

If I was wasting time,
if I was dirty,
if I was a good boy,
I couldn't say.
Someone was calling me
from far away,
but I didn't want to go inside.

That child isn't me
but the happy beast I once was
without knowing,
when I played beneath the song of cicadas
and the gold dimmed to dusk.
The time will come
when the night outside
will touch the night within,
and I might not have the chance
to say farewell to the flesh,
so I'll say it now,
not as an old man
or as a young man;
I'll say it while I'm just a man:

Goodbye, my tongue,
bed of spit,
rudder of my words.

Goodbye, my throat,
slender tunnel of breath;
you held nothing.

Goodbye to my mouth;
I never kissed you.

Goodbye, my skin;
no more caresses for you.
And my legs, where did
all that walking lead us?

Goodbye to the lids
of my eyes,
where night slips
into envelopes of sleep.

Goodbye to the dim
and deadly blossoms;
the tumor they wrenched from me
and threw away,
I never mourned you.

Goodbye to the shit
I exiled from my bowels
in lonely rooms, that shame
taught to me long ago,
the shame of being an animal.

Goodbye to the piss, the tears,
the sweat and snot,
the filthy rain I wrung from the rag of my flesh
but was, too, my flesh,
for a little while.

Goodbye to my sex,
perch of my lusts,
hoist of a song I heard
in uneven heaves of breath.

Goodbye to the shimmering threads
I cast from someplace deep in me.

Goodbye to the hands
that never lied to me.

My only body,
will you be lonely?
I'm not sure which of us
is really leaving.
Or perhaps we'll come together
so completely,
I won't be able to look at you anymore.

Goodbye to the parts of me
I could not touch,
liver and spleen
and heart,
the machines I never minded.

Goodbye to my shadow.

Goodbye to the well
of my hunger.

Goodbye to the labyrinths
of the blood.

JOHNNY LORENZ, son of Brazilian immigrants to the United States, was born in 1972. He received his PhD from the University of Texas at Austin and is currently an associate professor of English at Montclair State University. His poems, articles, and translations have appeared in a variety of journals and anthologies. In 2003, he was awarded a Fulbright grant to translate the poems of Mario Quintana. In 2013, he was a finalist for Best Translated Book for his translation of A Breath of Life (Um Sopro de Vida) by Clarice Lispector.

MARIO QUINTANA was born in 1906 in Rio Grande do Sul, the southernmost state of Brazil. He passed away in 1994. Author of more than twenty volumes of poetry and a regular newspaper contributor, Quintana was—and continues to be—one of the most beloved poets of Brazil. His volumes include A Rua dos Cataventos (1940), Espelho Mágico (1951), Caderno H (1973) and 80 Anos de Poesia (1986). In 1980, Quintana was awarded the Prêmio Machado de Assis from the Brazilian Academy of Letters.

www.ingramcontent.com/pod-product-compliance
Lightning Source LLC
Chambersburg PA
CBHW030454010526
44118CB00011B/933